across the light

Bruce Owens

Other Books by Bruce Owens

Quiet Places

Eddies in the Rush

A Passage Through Stone

Mend the Broken Branch

across the light

Bruce Owens

Middle Creek Publishing & Audio
Beulah, CO • USA

Books may be purchased in quantity and/or special sales by
contacting the publisher. All inquiries related to such matters
should be addressed to:

Middle Creek Publishing & Audio
9027 Cascade Avenue
Beulah, CO 81023
editor@middlecreekpublishing.com
(719) 369-9050

Cover Image: Bruce Owens
Cover Design: David A. Martin, Middle Creek Publishing
Printed in the United States
Author Photo: Courtesy of Bruce Owens

First Edition, 2017

ISBN: 978-0-9989322-4-8

*This book is dedicated to
my dear friend Kimberley Sokoloff,
who has been a constant gift of support.*

across the light

---

forward
iv

light from over the hill

3   I recently traveled across my fingerprints to
    the edge of the milky way
4   There is a voice so quiet
5   Almost
6   Wife
7   Dirt and green
8   I open the blouse of water
9   I can only touch you as I go
10 I came into the forest
11 Kiss her once and you will understand
    history
12 Coins
13 Jars full of fireflies
14 Delay the sky
15 I might just call this some kind of simple
    glory
16 And death
17 Pillow
18 Desert of the heart
19 If there was one moment I could keep
20 It passes
21 Breaking the heart
22 Birch
23 Small bird and bird bath

hollow with light

27   Buffalo head
29   Embrace
30   Child abuse
32   Someplace
33   Rome
34   Old woman mountain
35   Observation
37   Leaf mirrors adrift
39   I have gone so far now
41   Ruby throated hummingbird
42   Hippy gringo
44   Hero
45   Ghost among the boulders
46   Expressions
47   Empire sleeping
49   Rewind
50   The onset of alzheimer's
51   Stains

language of light

55   A flower
56   Amber
58   Be kind
59   Be not far from me
61   Black stone shining
62   Faith holds its small wings
63   I want to start something incredible
64   It was worth it all
65   Memory sails towards our dreams
66   Quiet within
67   Reflections
69   Taking a walk

minnows of light

75   Awakening

76   Childhood innocence

77   Doppler effect

78   Deserts of wandering

79   Dust and wind

80   Eidos

81   Evening crows

82   Flat rock

83   Ghost

85   Leaf

86   Ode to Robert Jeffers

88   Owls in the canyon

89   I am

90   In these quiet hills

91   Immense calm

93   Tonight I want to sleep close to the earth

94   Old stone

98   Sanderlings

100   Landscapes

101   Our bluebird song

102   No trespassing

103   too quickly

104   Evening

105   Minnows

Forward

I am not sure how I first connected with Bruce Owens, other than a serendipitous connection online through communication of mutual friends in the global poetry community, but there is no doubt of the moment I connected with his poetry. It was in the moments I was reading his poem, Wife.

Wife

A fox sniffs the edges of the woodlands.
Crickets are chirping in the tall grass.
Moons eye the ground,
casting clear light through the owl's eye
and branches of white oak.

A canopy of leaves throws shadows across your body
engraving your moist skin with an ancient design.

I pull your thighs across the slippery moss
into a cold, clear stream.
Our breathing becomes one;
a secret language of water
moving between stones.

The map of our hands;
a journey of transparent veins
drifting to the heart of a pond.

And I, the hunter, have found my own body,
as I tremble over your lips.

The crickets listen in the tall grass
to a horse that neighs in a distant field.

This poem snared me in its magic, and forced me to delve into more of Owens works. It was the gateway poem for me into his rich body of work, and has become one of my favorite poems of all time. For me it is a very personal connection. To me it functions as a counterweight to the burdens of the world. Argument can easily be made that it holds a companion place for me as Wendell Berry's poem The Peace of Wild Things does for so many. Although I wouldn't say that Wife exerts a force opposite of Berry's poem, it supports somewhat diametrically opposed moments, and each provides medicine or remedy for particular imbalances. A counter-weight by traditional definition provides balance and stability to a mechanical system, and its purpose is to make lifting the load more efficient. This poem can be seen to work in such a manner as it provides the balance and stability necessary to make the lifting of our daily load more efficient, and the endurance of our lives a little more enjoyable.

Each person enjoys a certain style of poetry, finding themselves partial to particular elements, even down to preferring particular structures, forms and content. There was just something about this poem, which I have read many, many times, that hit home much in the same manner that the poetry of Jim Harrison does for me, although it was written nearly 50 years before I discovered Bruce Owens and long before much of Jim Harrison's poetry was published. As I was working on editing and formatting the manuscript you now hold in your hands as a book, it occurred to me that a favorite line from Harrison *"A creek is more powerful than despair"* just might serve as an acorn-tight bridge I often find myself standing upon, and supported by the foundation provided by Owens' and Berry's poems mentioned above.

Wife is what I consider a pure, archetypal poem. It is a great poem of Human Ecology. Within it we find the natural and pastoral, a sense of place and moment, it is human enough to be both secular *and sacred.* It portrays the union of female and male, romantically celebrating fertility and the regenerative, reproductive and procreative Life Force couched in the terms of natural, active desire. The act of love is easily understood as mutual, and Owens lines showing rather than telling this with the quivering of the lips, the wet skin and the sliding of thighs, the couples two breaths becoming one, and the discovery of the narrators own body in the moments of connection to body of the other.

This is a poem of balance. Owens employs, not only an equanimity between the portrayal of it's elements or players, but justifies opposites in a most subtle, and well crafted manner. The narrator notes the crickets singing in the grass, attracting their mates with their chirps and that this is surely a mirror of what is occurring between the two lovers in that same moment due to it's proximity to lines concerning love making. The crickets then stop chirping and seem to perhaps now have become the listeners in the grass, trading places with the narrator in that aspect. It occurred to me as well that as the humans consecrate their love with their breaths becoming one and the sense of water flowing between stones, perhaps the crickets as well have stopped chirping as their mate has also arrived.

This is also a poem of space. We see this not only in the sense of smallness and largeness such as the smallness of the crickets in the tallness of the grass, but also in use of the sense of distance. We begin with a fox at *the edge* of a wood, and the relation of moon to the ground. We are given both light and darkness here with the moon and the owl, and a sense of space as the light moves between branches, branches of *white* oaks, no less, in the darkness. The moon-dappling of light silhouetting leaves creating patterns on the lovers skin infers that the area of skin is not small to accommodate and display such patterning, and almost subconsciously, we know that this wet skin is a naked body seen at a distance, most likely slight. We are given this vision and it places us there in close proximately to the lover. The space between the lovers now closes, and are treated to terms of water, liquidity, flowing, pooling, collecting, drifting. We are aware of the space between the couple and the crickets nearby, suddenly silenced and listening. A horse neighing in a distant field gives us an even further distance and moves the scene out further into an even more dimensional space, a space which is filled with the horses voice, bridging the distance.

This poem speaks of oneness, of form and formlessness, of the qualities of a moment and the timelessness therein, a union of opposites balanced within the field of the poem body. Each time I read it I find myself touched in a reciprocal manner, I am touching the poem and it is touching me back, I feel seen, even honored and know that the world is good, far beyond the ego, far beyond time and is a reassurance to me that the Love I love will live on and on. When Steve McVey says,*"For the first time, instead of being an outsider looking into a poem, I experienced what could only be called the transcendent sensation of being inside it."* I can completely sympathize. I feel that he may very well be referring to this very poem, as it is a poem that I find myself reading from a place within the poem itself.

As an outdoorsman who has spent the better his life in natural settings, contemplating and exploring much of the leitmotifs of this poem, I believe it to be a poem of high archetypal experience. There is a somewhat Taoist sense within its illuminated motif of simultaneous simplicity and interpenetrating complexity, its sense of emptiness and fullness, and an elegance to the interplay of the dark and the light. In this prize poem, Owens has skillfully managed to present a sense of balance between humans and Nature by employing a concise, almost minimalist approach to pastoral depiction. He does this to such a degree that humanity, within the poem, is a balanced part of nature. It shows the human spirit as belonging equally to the natural world as does the fox about its business, the crickets calling to their mates in the grass, and the horse neighing in the distance. It reflects Aldo Leopold's "land ethic" which, when propounded, inserted into the cannon of American Nature Literature the philosophy that humanity should not strive consider themselves rule Nature, but rather consider themselves an equal part of Nature and strive to harmonize with it.

I am reminded of the anthropologist and poet-philosopher Loren Eiseley who once wrote, "Man is always marveling at what he has blown apart, never at what the universe has put together, and this is his limitation." Bruce Owens' poem "Wife," when read, is remedy to the estrangement of the modern consciousness from Nature and a step toward alleviating humanities great spiritual crises and the cognitive limitations plaguing us due to widespread nature deficit disorder.

This poem well deserves a place in the great tradition of nature writing in American literature, as embodied in the work of such classic authors as Henry David Thoreau, Ralph Waldo Emerson, and John Muir, and modern writers such as Annie Dillard, Mary Oliver, Edward Abbey, Loren Eiseley, and many others. I am honored to be able to publish it, and it is my hope that this poem, along with the other poems of Across the Light and Bruce Owens himself, will receive due recognition and admiration.

David Anthony Martin
Founding Editor,
Middle Creek Publishing & Audio

light from over the hill

**I recently traveled across my fingerprint
to the edge of the universe.**

I recently traveled across my fingerprint to the edge of the universe.
I expect no one to understand this. I am not a Smart Phone dream.
I am not a digital summation.
I walk towards the sea and hear the sound of immensity.
I am translated in the moment by waves and stars overhead.
I am not your city or your metropolis.
The painted dolls of the empire pass by in dark Mercedes
and all the glamour light falls on them
and then the whisper of youth fades.

I am out here walking the beach with moonlight shining on me,
listening into the distant bark of seals.
Your cities march against themselves.
The masquerades are evident.
I take off my clothes and wade deep into the tumultuous sea.
The clouds pass by the moon and are signature to what is real.
No matter your resistance, the undertow of nature has you
and there is no insurance policy to protect you.
It is more the embracing of creation as it glides you home.

Bruce Owens

There is a voice so quiet

There is a voice so quiet,
a cricket climbs into it, and mimics the sound of a star. A mouse in the
wood pile, moves about, brushing the dark with whiskers... Her children
scurry after her into the woods. Nearby, the moon slips in over a pond
like a sheet of glass. The moon is full. Everything is so still. Just a twig
cracking...a chill winter wind . . .

Almost

You can almost
touch the breathing of your lover,
hear the ocean stirring in there,
where her life is drawn in
and breathed out.
You can almost
hear the surf lapping
on the shore of her dreams
while her heart drums softly.

Her nerves are threads of clear silk
embroidered into a cloud
that drifts above her skin.
You can almost see
the shadow of the cloud
as it sails into the harbor.

It is summer in her body.

The gold ring on her finger
glows like a sunset.
You can almost
wear it but the splendor of love
slips below the horizon
and the day leaves us
to memory that almost
allows us to catch what is lost.

Bruce Owens

Wife

A fox sniffs the edges of the woodlands.
Crickets are chirping in the tall grass.
Moons eye the ground,
casting clear light through the owl's eye
and branches of white oak.

A canopy of leaves throws shadows across your body
engraving your moist skin with an ancient design.

I pull your thighs across the slippery moss
into a cold, clear stream.
Our breathing becomes one;
a secret language of water
moving between stones.

The map of our hands;
a journey of transparent veins
drifting to the heart of a pond.

And I, the hunter, have found my own body,
as I tremble over your lips.

The crickets listen in the tall grass
to a horse that neighs in a distant field.

Dirt and green

The barn is heavy with silence
where the gold tobacco hangs.
A road cuts through the fields
like a thread of smoke:
a whir of wings, fireflies
above the slow rolling dark.
In my Grandmother's yard,
in every black tree,
there is the high-pitched hum of katydid
that rises and falls, the incessant chant
of their mating telecast
somewhere
up there
where the stars
blink through the branches.
At the hardware store
out on Hwy. 80
I told the young high school girl
I was from California.
Her eyes touched a daydream
way back in her mind.
I told her how beautiful
this part of Kentucky was.
"Boring, ya mean.
Nothin' but dirt and green!"
The cadence in her voice
carried the scent of honeysuckle
and the humidity of a summer day
just before a cloud burst of rain.
I entered her voice and let it carry me
over the freshly ploughed fields,
the glint of gold on the darkening ponds at dusk
when this part of the world goes silent.

Bruce Owens

I open the blouse of water

I open the blouse of water
unbutton the seeds of the melon

only to sleep in the yellow of the lemon

your hair falls down along my body
like a noon day shower

each drop of rain opens like a flower
each petal reminds me of your lips

I open the stone at midnight
and enter the dark
to pick the stars like berries

The waves at midnight are placed in a box
of rosewood and released in the morning
for Mary

I can only touch you as I go

I can only touch you as I go. All departures and arrivals in one moment
like a sacred perfume. You in turn touch me as you go, launched
in a ship carrying the gold of your dreams
but each touch before we go is a sunset in our eyes
and a smile, home, our children grown. So we dance together
across the ballroom floor not caring of the day before
or the night ahead. We just dance to the music of our heart,
knowing we are lovers till the end.

Bruce Owens

I came into the forest

I came into the forest
believing all the fairytales,
how the tress rose up at night and walked,
and that little people hid behind rocks until the moon
fell on their shadows
and made them skitter off like a flash of gold.
I believed the fish would jump out of the water,
and in mid-air, talked to one another.
I believed the stars were flowers that came down into
the forest to sleep with us for awhile, and that the dew was the tears
they left behind, when they ascended the stairs back up into heaven.
I believed the moss on the forest floor
was a place of dreams,
where I went to lay my head and sleep.
I recall, in my dreams angels came and looked
in on me, and smiled as they kissed my forehead,
and then disappeared, as light from over the hill began to fill the forest.
I believed all of this when I awoke and rose to yawn and stretch,
and look out my bedroom window
to the nearby forest just beyond the stream that was alive
and shinning with the early summer light.

Kiss her once and you will understand history

Kiss her once and you will understand history.

The second kiss will build into a house
The third kiss will bring the laughter of children.

I touch the hem of water
and it is music to the touch.

I touch her cheek in the night
and it is the warmth of silk spun from moonlight.

Our hands find each other
and we become one road in the night
wet with a fresh rain.

A child is a puzzle we put together
with each touch. Soon
we see the picture forming.

One relative at the house warming, whispers,
"She has your eyes."

Another says, "She has your fire."

I place the puzzle piece in place,
which is her small hand,
and then I fit together another piece,
which is her small mouth.
Soon she will be laughing
and playing with other children.

I am stunned by birth and life,
and the living.

Bruce Owens

Coins

I am counting my dimes slowly but first the pennies
that shine like autumn leaves in the forest...I will toss
the dimes up into the night sky and they will become stars
and the one quarter I have will shine like the moon rising over the hills
and the nickels I have saved I will give back to the lost tribes
who traded in abalone shells.
I will gather the wealth of water up in my hands
and give freely the pure gift of the mountain stream . . .

Jars full of fireflies

There are so many stars tonight. The treetops exploded with the light. Mystery is lingering everywhere. Listen. Do you hear the rumble of the galaxies . . . that soft and violent light . . . so far away . . . yet, so close, you can carry it in your hands like a jar full of fireflies, as you glide with the other neighborhood kids, laughing as you cross the deep lawns of childhood into the night that grows dark except for the small jars blinking with lights that grow smaller and smaller until they disappear beneath the trees in that landscape you knew so well, so many years ago . . .

Bruce Owens

Delay the sky

Delay the sky. Speak softly to the small birds.
Walk among your ancestors like one listening to the wind.
Wear the ocean like a silver ring.
Reel in a star and let it grow in your mind like a kiss.
Soon, it will be what has been
and the memory of your journey will be felt in the silence of the night.
Sip your coffee slowly and watch the faces passing by.
One day, they will beam at you
and give you a simple greeting like an angel
and God's glory will open up in you like a sunset
over the vast parries where the tall grass wavers with light.

I might just call this some kind of simple glory

I pass by our bedroom window.
It frames the glow of morning.

Out on the pond,
a turtle is crossing the still water.
The wild ducks paddle in calm circles.
Other birds fly in from their artic travels
and touch down on the wet shine
as the day breaks open
like your lips that want to tell me something.

I am at ease as I move, from room to room,
in this place with white walls shinning like prayer.
or perhaps I am simply sailing inside my own voice
in this place called prayer.
There is enough room in this place
for us to touch each others face,
to touch the language of the stars
in each others voice.

Outside the kitchen window,
there is a long billed hummer
that sings with rain in its throat
and takes pollen to other gardens, in other places
where the snow has melted and wild flowers
climb towards the sun.

We sit at the hard wood table.
You tilt your head as if to ask a question
and smile. Your long black hair is disarrayed
from the night before. I could live with that look
in your eyes forever.

I might just call this some kind of simple glory.

Bruce Owens

And death

And death.... sleeps on a quill
imagining a moon inside a wave of discourse
whereby one believes one thing
and one believes antihero thin ice sculptured from Syrian figurines
of her living face as if this is believing another thing.
It anchors in your frail angelica and the deep seething of a Bach trumpet
where deep speaks to deep the sky glides past pure music far beyond
all you ever imagined . . .

Pillow

I sit here in my own quiet,
listening into the space you once occupied.
It is only the indentation in the pillow next to me.
The soft round indentation where your head once laid and dreamed.
It has been weeks now since you were taken from me
and I dare not move the pillow lest I lose you forever.

Bruce Owens

Desert of the heart

I long for you…
your soul carving essence into my soul.

But we rose up through ourselves,
dislodged from ourselves
like boats in dry dock
longing for water.

I long for your face,
the scarf of wind
that has slipped the clutch of time.

What raged in us against simple love?
What snare tore us apart?

The helm is worthless
when the water is snatched from the ocean
leaving the rudder like a fin
to slash dry air in the immense desert
of the heart.

Your heart was the compass.
Your slender hands the helm
and your body was the light
that guided us through the night
Your eyes a gift of stars
for the soul to remember
the map and the journey
of each kiss that took us
to where memory is folded
into the wind
but now the rudder is a fin
that slashes dry air
in the immense desert of the heart.

If there was one moment I could keep

If there was one moment I could keep
it would be the summer I slept quietly
on a pillow of leaves, near the mummer of water,
near the mummer of dreams, and that one dream
in which I kissed you, all young and sweet
in that moment into which we can never again retreat,
lost like a sliver coin in the cool grass
that slipped down to the streams edge
where our destiny met
then sped away like the current of sleep
then sped away
and there it went
a whole life of living
in one moment spent

Bruce Owens

It passes

It passes...look at it all as you will. It passes.
The husband, the wife,
the leaves in the woods.
It passes. And your memory will linger
like a stream in the mountains
giving glory to the sea,
but, it passes. And all you have kept... photos pass
like your strength. But, there is the day he holds your hand,
wrinkled with the laughter of your life
and the thought of that will never pass
but live on through your grandchildren
and their children like a ship
forever sailing into the harbor of lights.

Breaking of the heart

Every night and day my heart breaks.
at the sight of a slender tree in the wind,
It breaks in the surf and in the dapple light of autumn leaves.
It breaks in the sound of my sleep where my voice
is trying to find the shore.
It breaks, this heart of mine,
in your eyes when you smile into me.
It breaks like thunder above a field where mice scurry.
My heart breaks at the trembling lips of pain
I do not wish to kiss
but I must embrace the grief of my heart to know
the shinning of things after the rain,
and endure the kiss of departures and the greetings
of friends both young, and old; the setting of the table for guest
or laying out silverware for two.
My heart breaks in all of this,
but it must break, and it is a good thing for it is the way
of life that marries the heart,
to hope that is stronger than the wind
or a storm on the open sea.

Bruce Owens

Birch

A face swirls off boulders
into a stream,
runs the clear current
till it spills
off,
drifts

to become a still pool
reflecting clouds
and branches of white birch

Small bird and bird bath

A small bird was getting wet in the bird bath.
There was song in the garden.
Who was singing the bird or the water?

hollow with light

Buffalo head

He wanted to walk off into the frontier,
slip into the sheen of a crow,
and fly, tunnel under the prairie grass,
and disappear into the moist night,
listening under ground
to the stampeded of buffalo overhead.

All he wanted was to follow the evening
flow of the Sweetwater, become a shadow
among the stones, count shooting stars forever.

These notions were soon abandoned,
as they built a saloon out in the middle of nowhere.
Then they laid a spur of track out across the dust
so tourist could shoot buffalo from the windows of the train.
The local Indians posed for photographs
with their newly adopted friends.

The saloon was full of smoke, and smelled of whiskey.
Bowler hats hung on hooks, and women folk
hung onto their bloomers,
and some men folk hung from the gallows
that swayed with heavy shadows.

The Sweetwater mirrored the arrival of clouds in slow bends
from Devil's Gate as far as the eye could perceive West.

They would never find the reflection of his face
as he leaned over the water. No one
would photograph his eyes as they peered down
into the quiet depths of the Sweetwater.

Bruce Owens

This is all he wanted
when he walked into the frontier;

this was payment enough
to reach down and touch the river running clean.

No buffalo head hanging above
the saloon door to bring him peace.

Embrace

We embrace that which we do not want to let go of
If the dead could only return to our open arms
If autumn leaves aglow with the touch of earth
Would fly up to the startled branches
And once more fill the trees with emerald light
And winter light would retreat into the silence
Of the hills, where boulders break
The will of the wind

Bruce Owens

Child abuse

I tried to follow my name but only ate
the gravel of a lone road near the wolf's cry
along a dusty ridge. What did I go there to see?
Was it my mouth's thirst for water that shapes the moon
rising over the hills?

What is it that searches in me for water?

To be born of earth, to speak with children,
to carry a rose up the hill to touch the setting sun,
to loosen the skirts of rain,
to fly all night in a dream,
to unravel the mystery in the owl that haunts my memory.

What should I say
about my childhood…that I was tortured day and night
and locked in closets where the dark creatures made me scream
as my step grandmother guzzled gin
on the other side of the door where light shined.
I wept and pleaded and then poured myself into a whimper.

What is it in me that searched for water?

To be born of a flower in a field of wild flowers,
to capture light like a window, to be a flame aglow
above a row of candles in the quiet cathedral of the heart,
to be a prayer that unlocked the closet door of my childhood,
to be free at last from torment and those that torment the innocent.

I was only eight years old when she shut me up
in the tight dark of that closet space.

To be a stream in the woods that mirrors the trees,
to be the autumn and then to be the snow,
to find that lucky penny in the nick of time,

to be translucent as a leaf,
to find the water, I searched for all my life,
to wear the ocean like a dream,
to find my name
and know myself as one that is loved.

Bruce Owens

Someplace

We were in the yard,
near the sky,
on a place
we called home.
The house leaned into the wind
and groaned with each storm.
There was a familiar tilt to the front porch,
yet it was all caught in a strange snag of time
like the clothes that flapped on the line in the summer heat.
Comfort came to us in neat packets.
Every Monday the milkman delivered
thick bottles of pasteurized milk.
The slow clouds touched the hills with shadows;
white sheets cool with evening, the whir
of the living room fan on the other side
of the screen door.

Behind the house,
the woods drifted down to a trickle of a stream.
The woods concealed our sins.
It was there
in the silence that hummed overhead,
we sliced our fingers with a pocketknife
and said our blood pack of endless friendship.

The sight of blood made my head hollow with light
and for a moment I seemed to travel
someplace I'd never been,
somewhere between the light and the dark.

32

Rome

A whole civilization
tilts over
in the woods
and sinks in the dark
near the sound of the creek.
There is the deep chugging of engines,
then all is silent.

Standing over the spot,
I peer down
through
the damp duff of the woods;

a few soft lights are still blinking
in the depths like
some mute creature
refusing to die.

Bruce Owens

Old Woman Mountain
(Kodiak Island)

In the clear distance
I see mountain peaks
covered with the white shawls
old women left
when they passed from this world
into the next

Observation

She likes to drive up the coast
to a café where they bake blueberry muffins
and sip on hot coffee. Outside at a table
there is an enclosed patio with a view
of the ocean. On weekdays in winter,
there are very few people; mostly locals.
Sometimes, foreigners slip in past the screen door
and peer around inside the café
like they are visiting a small, rare cathedral.
At one time the café was a roughneck bar
with peanut shells on the floor, a place
where field workers, cow pokers, bikers
wearing black leather and tattoos on their necks,
would come and vent their machismo.
Now the place had been converted into a subdued
tourist trap with an expensive menu.
I didn't care for the new ambiance but missed
the Saturday night brawls, the loud and lewd women,
the bloodshot eyes of the Mexicans sipping
on a bottle of beer and tossing peanut shells on the floor.
Back then the place had character
like an old Clint Eastwood movie, but now
it was like the flat shiny menu with no rough edges.
Some things never change. Outside at the tables,
small blackbirds flocked. They were bold
and dropped in right next to your plate,
and hobbled back and forth
waiting for a hand-out. They cocked their small
shinning heads with evil yellow eyes and gave you
the once over look.
So we tossed a piece of the blueberry muffin at our feet
and watched them flit to the ground.

Bruce Owens

The signature of the pecking order instantly manifested itself.
One blackbird
was encircled by the other birds
waiting for a chance to snatch the prize.

I was reminded of the brawls at the bar back
in the late 60's and knew that the bar had been
glossed over with a new look and a new menu,
but just under the surface, the old pecking order
remained in tack.

Leaf mirrors adrift

Where can I find you Lorca
asleep among the poppies of snow
that grow next to her skin
A candle glows
in the middle of a stream
flowing towards her lips
You kiss the rose
and gently toss it
into the sea
Spain
at war with itself
did not know how
to strum her long undone hair
the color of dusk or the shine
of a crows wing

They did not know how to fly into her
low hills, the trees, a silhouette of eyelashes
closing on the cafe lights
where you read her this poem
sipping spring water from the palm of her hand.

Like the rifle smoke after the execution,
you staggered off, your white silk shirt
stained red
and where you fell
no one knows
where you left you dreams...

Some of them drifting down the Hudson
like leaf mirrors.
Other having found harbor in small towns
like moths around a porch light

Bruce Owens

And maybe one dream was clutched in Hart's hand
before he leaped overboard

And the goons that killed you
outside your friend's house,
the goons that dragged you out into a field,
jeered you and called you a Fag

But now, some sixty years later,
I touch your green words in the tower of the wind
and my hands on the balcony
as I look out into the world,
the green, green world…

I have gone so far now

Silence
breaks open like seeds
and scatters
in sound.

The tin lit wind
lashes
fireflies against scars
scratched into the dark trunk of oaks.

The trail of a snail's silk glitters
on a leaf.

The moon is the white meat of walnuts,
fillet of shadows,
fluting in the thin water of a stream.

Pale.
On the hill.
Morning comes. Wet.

Without words, I watch
the wind in worn stones.

Horses.

Hour deep in the thinking.

Tall grass growing just beyond sound.
I hear a swish of the tail
brush the sun.

Bruce Owens

Coming into the full length of my arms,
a warm, moving mixture in veins,
red ripening in leaves,
fallen at my sides:

north and south

Ruby throated hummingbird

I saw a ruby throated hummingbird hovering in the rain, then darting at light speed without fear into the storm and disappear into the invisible. I set my umbrella down and began to flap my arms. I wanted to follow the hummingbird, which had no fear, into the deep dark wild wind. Suddenly, I became a rainbow on the other side of the storm, arched over the green hills, glowing with invisible joy.

Bruce Owens

Hippy gringo

Then there was
a voice that found me
when I was
alone
with no voice
and no home
and all I had was
that which I carried.
The soles of my shoes were thin
as a worn dime, dull
with no shine at all.
My pants were thread bare
and when I awoke in a field
off on the side, away from the tracks,
I found black ants crawling in my hair.

The train had stopped in the middle of the night,
in the middle of no where in particular.
I had clamored down from a boxcar
and found a place on the ground to sleep.
In the early hours before light, I heard the train
jerk alive and begin to rattle slowly at first until
it clip clopped away
and then sleep took me.
When I awoke and brushed the ants from my hair,
there was no train, only soft rolling hills in the distance,
the hum of green fields.
A small fist of fear clenched into the shape of my heart.
Off in the distance, a cloud of dust was
coming my way and with it my destiny.
I did not know this. Who can?
The dust was from a truck driven by local field hands

hired to fix the track. When they saw the hippie
with pack and all, they had a good laugh, and fired
a barrage of rapid Spanish my way. I just looked on
with the look of one that has lost his way. They laughed
a little longer, then patted me on the back,

and the tall one with a big hat, spoke to me in English,

the words spaced out, and sort of weighed before spoken.
He smiled, showing two silver teeth, and told me
not to worry. They would be working the track
and the next train would slow down, as they repaired the rail.

They all waved goodbye, as I hopped into
a slow moving boxcar with sliding doors on both sides
wide open to the view of the shinning ocean
and the fields, rolling hills,
and those five polite Mexicans waving their hats,
and grinning at the funny gringo kid.

The open door of the boxcar was like a widow
that framed the scene in my mind forever.

The Mexican men with the backs of their shirts, sweat stained,
pesky flies, an unbearable noonday heat,
the sound of distant surf is still with me, years later.
These men opened the clench fist of fear
the way a flower opens in the morning,
and their laughter, and wide grins
gave me back my voice,
and I thank them.

The train took me to a small coastal town
called Guadalupe.
Near the tracks is a graveyard
and a four way stop.

Bruce Owens

Hero

They interview the war hero.
They never interview a lion after his meal.
The warrior is praised and medals hang from his chest.
They speak of his humility.
They speak of his great sacrifice.

I want to speak of the humility
of the child cowering in the corner of a mud hut
with a fly on his lip, quivering at the passing of soldiers,
some wearing turbans, others wearing helmets.
There are no medals of honor dangling
above his pounding heart, yet he dared to go out
and seek water for his dying sister
and wiped the face of his mother with his dirty sleeve.
No one saw the landmine that blew him
into the next kingdom.

I want to pin a medal of honor above his little heart.
Death kissed him,
and his life passed like the shadow of a dream.

Those eating strawberries, do not lament his passing
or hear the mothers wailing as they kneel on the ground,
flinging hands full of dirt up into the air
like they were tossing their dried tears
up into heaven.

Ghost among the boulders

Li Ho, who lived over a thousand years ago,
and wrote verse, and sold his embroidered silk
for a cup of wine to null his poverty.

His name shines like green bamboo,
or like a mountain peak with the light of dusk.

His feudal China has disappeared,
and is among the ghost in the cold boulders
that have rolled down to the rivers edge.

The village where he was born is covered with mounds of grass,
and has been erased from the new maps
of a communist geography.

A boy, he wrote, once coveted an iron arrowhead.
The boy and the arrowhead are rust of a pointed leaf
that traces the silences.

Twelve centuries later, I arrive late to his verse.

What remains and what is lost forever.

Bruce Owens

Expressions

"...of course we know that our body is
an expression of something, but it takes a long time
to see clearly how and of what."
~George Teng

My body is folded into a leaf
that changes with the seasons:
a green, a gold, a black ring of the sun.

My body breathes an ocean at night,
and dreams. Each cell of my body
laps like a small wave at the shoreline of light.
The eyes of this body are cast like dice
onto a mountain meadow at first sound of spring.
The hands, my hands climb the air looking
for clues that will lead to the gates of this body.

Enter this body with caution. An entire city
lives within this body. This body
is the inhabitation of a multitude of citizens,
some crazed, some are ill, others filled with greed
live in the citadel of the skull, and still others
have escaped the rigors of the appetite,
and have found sanctuary in the cathedral of the heart.

Who can understand the resilience of the body?
It endures mountain passes, stumbling over boulders
in a rain forest among the bright bromeliads, Harlem in summer,
Prague in winter; fever and cold.
But for how long can it endure
the endless hum of solitary confinement?
And one deadly bacterium can take down the whole house,
subdue the entire city in its skeletal scaffolding.

46

Empire sleeping

The ponies will ride the wide spaces
where aromatic wisps flower

The poppies will spill into a gold coin
that rolls along the edge of the horizon

The morning will peep into a mirror
and slip into the damp gowns
that govern the shadow of trees

The cars will stop the incessant chase to nowhere

The wars will ceasefire and sleep
forever in the sounds of a rainforest
where the fluted throats of birds catch on fire

No cell phones will hum
No tigers in cages
The zoos will release the wild
No guns for children
Playgrounds will increase
No abuse only kindness
All the neighbors will greet each other
There will be no enemy
The State will dissolve in a bowl of Jell-O
No more taxes
No need for parking meters
Sirens in the night will cease
Prostitutes will marry their John
Third World hunger will sing with wheat in their hands
Gold will have the value of snow
No electricity in the computers
and digital will go analog like waves

Bruce Owens

lumbering towards the shore like a lullaby,
as the Empire goes to sleep and gently grazes
in a moon lit meadow

Rewind

Blue Jay out on the wood rail next to the roses
I am in here
listening
to Simon and Garfunkel
Forty years from there to here
Thousands of people have gone in and out
of my life, countless wars
Rebel CEO's in winter coats
She was my lover and in her name I sleep
like a dream that takes form in a storefront window.
I wave at the reflection and move on
to the next name and the next lover
Waving down a Cab
Handing my ticket to the woman in the booth
Walking a deer trail into the woods at night fall
or along a sandy cove, the still water alive with light
Who can speak and when you punch out your last cigarette
You sit alone in the dim lit room with the radio going
Then an old song comes on
Listening into your memories
Smile that sad and humorous smile
and laugh
at the fun you had when you were young and easy
No IRS taxman, no foreclosure, no iPad, no ma, no pa, nothing at all,
just your naked body free at last,
a signature of your life written into the wind.
But now it all has come home, the white hair, friends that are gone
or disappeared, the ache in your body that remains all night.
You never thought your nightstand would be lined with medications.
That was your grandmother's room, years ago, when your mother
took you to see her for the last time. All you remembered were
her glazed over eyes, a faint blue, and the smell of urine and mothballs.
How could this be you? Something in you wants to press: Rewind.

Bruce Owens

The onset of alzheimer's

What do we do now Study your hands all night How they open
and close and then open in the lamp light...
They say he fell today and broke his hip.
You care but then you think you too are slipping
down the dark walls of a quiet well
like a coin in a dream.
You see your life gliding down in the glitter of a quiet
only those growing older know and you reach over to touch something
forgotten in that dream and polish a memory
and then let it go.
You smile at the frailty of the music in your mind
that is a filament of a butterfly wing worn now
but still trying to flicker on and fly to the other side of the room
which takes all the effort of your arms and legs
to cross over to the light switch.
So you sit in the dark and listen to the music in your mind
and do not move for hours like a photograph on the wall
the grandchildren will look at in the years to come.
You have forgotten your name and the sky has no name
but is something that makes you smile all day long...
to be smiling with a cat on your lap but you only feel the purr
and warmth of the sun coming through the window
and somehow your thin legs have been covered with a blanket
when they wheel you out into the green yard
to listen to the birds.
You blink up at the sunlight.
Each breath is folded into a whisper...
your whole life is folded into a whisper
like the wind in the upper branches of the trees,
whose names you no longer remember.

Stains

Some of us
Are between two or three worlds
There is so much weeping here
I cannot find one leaf
That is not stained
By tears

language of light

Bruce Owens

A flower

A flower is its own kingdom, swaying
with the wind... hear how it prays,
asking for nothing. Yet
water from cool springs
shoots up its slender stalk
like a smile.

The flower in its tower of splendor
is never lonely. The bees visit all day,

gathering grain to pollinate
the world with mystery.

At night, the petals are small hands
that fold in on themselves and dream.

This is when the flower grows eyes
to see the moon high above
sailing with the clouds.

This is when the flower forms a mouth
that glows with new words never before spoken.

This is when the flower talks to other flowers.
Their heads leaning together,

sharing revelations,
as they go over manuscripts by the Master,
murmuring over the script that glows
inside the dew.

Bruce Owens

Amber

All day I stumble into myself.

Sometimes good, sometimes bad.

What stopped me was the blind woman
waiting for the bus,
the way she stood there unafraid,
leaning on the sunlight,
the warmth in it spreading across her face.

I placed myself nearby.
I needed her conversation.
I wanted to enter the quiet of her shadow
and wait with her for God.

We both knew he was coming
and was already here.

She was young and polite.

As we both waited for the bus.

I said, "It is a beautiful day."

As I walked deep
Into my self
imagining
how she saw the day.

Her reply was gently,
reaping sound in a small
stream
of silence

"Yes, it is quite lovely."

That is when
I saw the beauty in it,

the skull burning out to its final glory,
the way her hand dipped into
the surrounding air,

reaching in to touch the quiet fire
that will turn the leaves of autumn

to gold and amber.

Bruce Owens

Be kind

At times
you will sit
with those
who only love their hands, their purse,
their lips, and a mirror.
Be still
They are only waiting at a table
in some cafe
to breathe your breath
Be kind to them
for even the weeds drift
to where the wild flowers grow.

Be not far from me

old crow, black as the rain that shines.

What syllables are those
caught in the dark ruby caw
of your harsh throat;

your short rapid calls?

Your wings lumber upward,
carrying the winter light,
into the stark tree
to join your brother crow.

Throw down to me
the prayer of your kind,
as I glance up to where you perch.

Let me stand pure and clean
in your holy church,
where no preacher's climb, and each limb
and branch are scripture enough and shine.

I weary of their doctrine, the lack
of love. For love has already
split the tomb from above.

Be not far from me,
old crow.
The light is faint along the horizon glow . . .

Bruce Owens

I need you old friend.
I need the broken syllables in your caw
as I lift up in flight

before the dusk shuts down
on the horizon
with night

Black stone shinning

Walking along Waddell Creek,
a rain starts to sweep in from the ocean.
I spot a small, round black stone.
It glows with its own light.
It has its own music,
There is a magnum opus
about to break out
within the black stone.
To be alone
within this black stone is to touch
the shadow of reality.
Within the stone some stars are beginning to shine
and the cosmos is slowly exploding outward.
I look up and a thin slice of rain
falls on my face.

No one knows the meaning of the black stone
lying alongside the slip of creek
with its winter drive.
The same force that formed the stone
is the same force that drives the creek.
I have been encountered just as I have encountered
I am satisfied to have known the stone,
the moment it held and this time in winter.

Bruce Owens

Faith holds its small wings

Faith folds its small wings into a white piece of drawing paper
and waits on the flat table by the window.
It is surrounded by crayons and colored pencils.

Faith remains calm and does not move when a light breeze through the
window stirs the room. Then a child climbs up onto a chair and takes
some of the crayons to draw a moon rising over a hill on the paper
where faith has folded its small wings. The little child is so happy and
laughs as the moon continues to rise above the hill and light shines into
a meadow clearing where deer are crossing. The child reaches towards
the paper to pat the deer and touch the glitter of snow in the meadow.

Faith has been at work all along unfolding its small wings to fly into the
cathedral of the child's heart, who has grown sleepy now, as she climbs
down from the chair...

I want to begin something unbelievable.

I want to begin something unbelievable.

Take a mountain inside my chest
and breathe the water inside the granite stars.

Who began me will end me like wheat reaching for the sky.
I will return to the place where autumn begins.
October will circle my heart with an orange fire.

I want to sleep inside a kitten's mute meow
and sing on the glide of a leaf
and to sing all night without fear
and listen to the mating calls throughout the woods
while the human creatures sleep their dreams.

I want to drift rootless like clouds over landscapes
of poppies and sand and clear lakes that mirror the sky.
It is here, at night under the stars,
I will close my eyes
and meet the lips of love again.

I want to begin something unbelievable.

Pull on a thread and unravel the mystery of the night
and believe, one more time, that peace is attainable.

Bruce Owens

It was worth it all

To say the moon is round as an orange is to travel around the sun in the
orchard at noon with the bees humming something

said that only bees know how to say

To say the ocean is water is to take a tear from the cheek
of a child whose father never returned from sea
to fill the boy's mind with tales of storms

Deckle me dumb or kettle me blind but do not throw stones at the worn
weather around the house with windows
wearing shades to riddle the hymn

Something sweet is something to delete like the growl of a bird about to
bark at the dog's meow in the yellow night
with the leap of black and bristle of fur to mix and confuse
and confess the fact that nothing is exactly like that

Do not bother to condemn me for this is what I need to say
and now that is has been said and does not need to be read I say go
out from here and sail this past your dream of tiger eyes
and spinning wheels of festive sparks to see
it was worth it all just to be

Memory sails towards our dreams

When our heads touch the pillow after a long day
there is the soft rise and falling of our breathing,
and in that sound little boats of memory sail
towards our dreams
that have a sound of their own
like a wind moving with dark swells
on another ocean
with its own time.

Bruce Owens

Quiet within

for Robinson Jeffers

The years I spent
escaping from under your shadow, Jeffers,
that glided over me
like the great wing of the hawk.
In my youth, I was caught by your vision,
but my pride fought off the claws of your words
that snagged my soul. Now I return,
somewhat glad for the traces of prophecy
that gild your thought like the set sun on the Pacific
that gilds the cypress and the pines of Carmel.
That high flicker of youth has burned the candle down
into a quiet reflection in myself. I argued Christ
with you, and my verse fought back at your vision of God.
Now, a deeper surrender, as my wry grin
fades in the mirror like the last light at sunset
fades from the stone house you built so many years ago.

I now wander into the hills and lie down to sleep
with the shadows, and the moon over my body, glowing clean.
I walk at dusk with those slender trees, never to be captured
by man or his dream, and let the roots of my feet
slip into an icy stream. I lived long, down in the city,
and gagged on chemicals, and a synthetic vision,
a digital empire empty from within; a Wasteland
of lights awash in a spiritual death.

Yet Jeffers,
I come back to you, and smile
at the windfall of apples in the orchard,
and I surrender to all that returns to mother,
and all that is quiet within us.

Reflections

The river is a long mirror
of shimmering
April light.

In the upper leaves of willows,
bay, and oak,
the language of light lingers in the rustle of wind
and below they dapple the shadows
where shallow water flows.

Crows color
the wind and cackle in the high branches.

The river ripples against iridescent green boulders.
There is a quiet here that goes undetected.

The silence hums.

Three ducks are signature
to the moment in the flow
of the river that mirrors
the trees along the banks.

Lazy like the afternoon,
the bees
excite the blooms.

I am the consciousness of nature
in these reflections.

Bruce Owens

I believe in all of this.
I am the mirror of light, shadows, silence,
leaves and the afternoon.
I am the lazy flow of water.
I am the bees that excite
the flowering acacia.

All of this believes in me
as I drift along
in this signature of my life.

If this were not true, wisdom
would not have given me candled eyes
to see with inside my head.

Talking a walk

As I go out the door
I wonder what I wished for.
Maybe it was nothing.
I desire to be free somehow, free
of this body, free of the phone, free of the mail,
free to just walk, spy out a flower or two,
look up into that big sky overhead, and try
to remember what the clouds are called
as they scurry their way
with no worries, only
storms in their bellies.
There on the porch is the cat,
the cat that always
seems to be there this time of day
where the sun is warming a splotch on the neighbor's porch.
I hear the piano lessons being given
inside the house.
The missed notes are returned to until
mastered by the young pianist.
The small fingers are remembering the notes
as if they were reading Braille inside the sway of wind.
I stop a moment in the shadows of the sidewalk.
The cherry blossoms are in bloom.
I listen into the music
that shapes my mind
into a dream.
The cat on the porch yawns in the sunlight.
A small wind catches the sound
of the distant surf pounding the cliffs.
I listen carefully now

Bruce Owens

as if it all depends upon what I hear:
the piano, the surf, the rustling of leaves,
children laughing somewhere, a door closing,
And all that I hear is a wonder of sorts,
and then someone calls out my name.
They seem to be calling from a distance,
and I am walking towards their calling.
Yes, I hear them calling. All my friends
are calling. The ones that have left are calling
and I can see each and every face
of those I played with and fought with
in that long ago playground.
Yes, I hear them calling
And what I hear is a wonder of sorts.

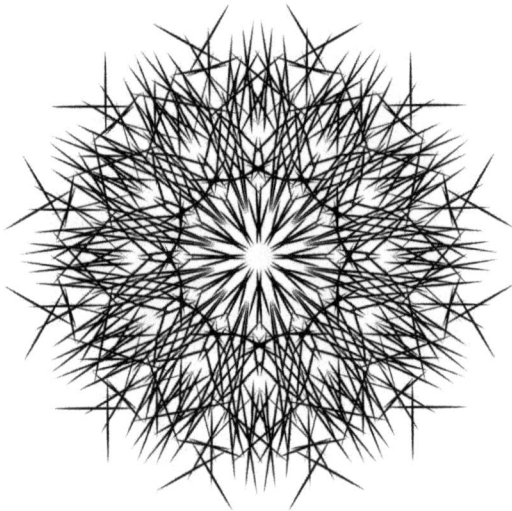

minnows of light

SHADOWS OF LIGHT

Awakening

It was late.
I could not find my bones.
They had become like blades of grass
lost in the drift of night
or like leaves that had fallen
quietly as a shift in season.
The marrow of my bones was like a frozen stream
slipping thru the woods; a dark signature
of my life that for many years slept in the meandering
light of autumn turned to a winter blaze of ice.
I did not comprehend the thaw of Spring
and that a deeper current always was
the truth of my life because fear was my tormentor
etched into a clear mirror
and I burned in that cold blaze
and I had memorized that fire of ice.
But the thaw has unleashed a joy
and the signature has awaken to light.
The flesh never could truly tarnish the spirit I am
because Spirit had given birth to spirit
and that life lives eternally within the deeper flow
of who I am.

Bruce Owens

Childhood innocence

All day
we went exploring
under
every cool rock
in the meadow
near the horses
that gave us
long unconcerned looks
as their tails swished in the morning.

We entered the grass
where shadows bruise the white cheek
and each blade is a green match
striking the earth with flame.

Sunlight cut through the slats
in the ceiling of the old barn.
Moats glittered in the openness.
Inside each moat was a stellar choir.

We climbed the rungs to the loft.
I touched the shine on your face.
Both of us not knowing what to do,
rubbed noses like the Eskimos

or like bees with furry bodies,
we rubbed against the soft gold of pollen.

Doppler effect

The smell of pavements was steaming that summer.
The orchard was heavy with light.
Hip-high weeds in the field hummed with insects.
Inside the barn leaning with decay,
a mouse looked up
and blinked at the light.

In the secret treehouse,
we fingered at her flat blouse.
We fought with small fists
as summer, fast, slipped away without sound.
We set sail paper boats
on black puddles lit by lightning.
Leaves fell
in space in time
in this
out of that
world
I knew like my neighborhood block.

Around the corner,
the train, sleek as a blade of flowering green...

the distant whistle
faded away,
God.

Deserts of wandering

It is not only man's own life that he fears,
but the way the body gets up in the morning
to dress in front of a mirror.

The wind in the trees is alright to watch,
but the wind out of the lung at night
is a mist with reason.

When I see a boy carrying school books,
I think of a black and white photograph
of my body standing in its eight years of growing,
and tear at the imaginary edges,
so my image can get free of time.

This woman who wipes my lower parts
with a dark scent,
has already gone into the future
planned to be the future,
and never will measure the exact size of this tongue
already gone back into a closed mouth.

Everything threads the sand,
wandering over the desert,
looking for water.

Dust and wind

The ocean inside these
my two small breasts
leaps when you come with
your moist gift of fire,
your transparent presence
more beautiful than almonds,
your skin, olive deep,
electrical to touch,
your eyes, the easy shade of trees
my eyes rest in.

We stroke the thin silence with
our bodies.
Small sounds break in
our throats.

At last we enter the warm ocean
inside each of us,
enter the slow thunder
inside of the mountain mysteriously formed
by the same love that formed us
from dust and wind.

Bruce Owens

Eidos

They say that Plato went about
trying to catch birds with his mind.
I kneel at this kind of beauty: one planet, then three planets
is the sum of four planets that circle the sun.
He was near heaven's
seven doors opening onto that which is bright.

But here the evening turns to shadow
and the trees have no form.
The mountain enters the deep star-calm of the lake
that mirrors a meteor shower glowing like a flare from a match.

I warm my hands by the edge of the campfire;
the embers burn in my mind like the summer and the night.

What did I bring to this spot in the Sierra?
What will I carry away? What remains?

I too go around trying to catch birds with my mind.

Evening crows

There were hundreds of them, crows
like a black tornado
over the wetland, rising up into the trees,
this orchestrated crackle, dispersing
to different branches assigned to their flight
and perch in the evening light;
this communal gathering, this ritual
of evening crows gathering in their black robes,
their throats afire like rosary beads
in the divine cathedral of the unseen;
the will that drives them
is the pure translation of music . . .

Yet, something seemed to disturb them
as they sat in the tall branches,
maybe the wind, I could not tell,
but they swooped down,
and rose again
in a black funnel of feathers,
and their caw-caught voices shined with caution;
ominous as storm clouds,
a brooding in their flight,
they climbed the air again, and then spread out
among the tree tops,
among the gossip,
these children with black eyes,
and blue-black-rain-sheen feathers,
these black knights with wings
that fly.

Bruce Owens

Flat rock

A flat rock in the desert captures a pool of light.
I lower myself into the water and spread out.
There is no one here to witness this mirror
I have become as sky slips in over me.
This place of light is far out in the silence of desert.
A live rain sweeps across my face. I am
living without distance, without time:
a flat rock capturing water and light.
At night my eyes stand still. The moon
tracing the depth of my transparent face
lingers as light: stars on the surface
of what I have become
will disappear in the morning
like this life.

Ghost

I walked slowly into the living room the way
I would imagine that a ghost walks.
This same living room my grandfather walked
into in the winter of 1928. The windows were sheets of ice
that winter, and in the streets in town, hoof prints
froze in place like a black, and white photograph.

His face is up on the mantle in an oval frame,
with those black eyes staring out into this era like the coal
he use to shovel down in the basement. He was
a man's man, a chip out of granite, squared chin,
and a charm with the ladies, until my grandmother's
charm tamed him into a malleable horse that snorted
over the newspaper at the kitchen table.

Grandfather loved to fish, and as a child of nine,
I loved the way
he untangled my fishing line, a bundle of nylon knots,
smoking a pensive pipe, the flat lake lapping at the edge
of nowhere in time, the clear nylon between his fingers,
and I thought I would look up, and see him
against a grey sky forever, tenderly untying my snag.

When she died, he refused to go fishing. He refused
to read the newspaper, refused to eat or even drink coffee.
I would drive over, and sit with him for hours,
saying nothing. Everything needed to be said was said
by the way he held her favorite scarf in his lap, the one
she wore when they walked the shores by the lake.
I wanted to reach over an untie my grandfathers grief
the way he untied my bundle of knots. I wanted
the clear nylon to unravel mysteriously in my hands

the same way it unraveled in his, but I could not
take the pain out of his eyes.

Now that he is gone, there is no one to take the pain
out of my eyes nor unravel the mysteries shipwrecks
all around me in this living room in winter

with all his things in place exactly the way he left them.

Leaf

When they
change the genetic code
so that the leaves will not
fall in autumn, our voices
will forget the piles of
burning leaves and
the discarded rake
will gather spider webs
in the tool shed. There
will never again be the sound of
crunching leaves
while walking with the favorite dog
through the woods at dusk.
People will line up early
at the doors of the museum
to catch a glimpse of a leaf exhibition.
There will be black-market dealing
in rare leaves and only
the very wealthy will be able
to eye them in private.

What a surprise it will be
to open an old book
and pressed between the pages,
the skeletal dust of a leaf.

Ode to Robinson Jeffers

They took the old road south into the fog.
The Scotchman was whiskey wise and full of tales.
He shook the reins in that wild sure footed trot
to deliver the mail by way of coach.

They speak how Jeffers labored with stone,
and built the stone tower for his Una, and young lads.
His Una is gone. Just the remnant of his consciousness
remains here with us, and a few of the cypress,
once small sprouts between his stained fingers.
As we saunter past his squat house
or outcropping of granite on that headland;
the garden is lazy with flowers: lupine, purple sage, and light
by the weathered gate. At night the moon out there
on the immense water rising and falling slowly
with the drift of swells.
Only a few stones in the millenniums to come
will be standing as the sun burns towards
its pithy black core

The day they took the old road into the deep fog
where even the hawks cry is mute, a sinister feel of the coast bit
backwards into his soul and something more pagan than Ireland
burned in his mind. But who remembers from day to day
the walking and the crossing over into something new
each moment as the honeysuckle sags with rainfall.
All these concerns never burned in his mind,
but something made him pit his strength
against the god out there
locked between the star, and stone.

He thought to be alone as he struck a match
to smoke, and gazed with wonder
at a meteor shower or moon on the tide waters.

The quilt on the steel framed bed on which he died
is cold as sea boulders below his house of stone,
and his vision is hemmed in by the poverty
of tenements built by the wealthy
that block the view of the ocean,
lock it out with their self contained demons.
Who will recall his words in the millenniums to come
after the earth, and the living God
has had its way with our kind?
Will science have caught up to greed
or will there be another Hiroshima?
In a thousand years how many stones will be
standing of his house by the Pacific water in Carmel,
once a village with a mail coach that went into the immensity
of the big south touched by high sea walls,
and the wail of birds both hawk and others?

Jeffers had hawks with broken wings,
and saw our kind as incestuous lovers of ourselves.
He never flinched at the naked real
dark, and wild eye of his god nameless, and cruel,
but not cruel because cruelty is only gnarled dust
in packages of charged neuronal abstractions,
swarms of bees around the frontal lobe: the new cortex
is the thin eggshell of an expanding empire. Let us be reminded
that a couple extra genes is what distinguishes our kind.
Better to sign with the hand and cross oneself ,
sprinkled the head with holy water amongst chants and candles
as Milosz hinted than touch an inhuman vision
Jeffers took for wisdom
the way a tide-pool catches stars in the stun, cold ocean
at the feet of the small cliffs by his house.
What we are is not debatable

but then again that superfluous excess in nature at sunset
does indeed touch a tender string in the soul.

Owls in the canyon

There are deer in the night.
I cannot see them but hear
the cracking of twigs, the snap of a branch
the scruff across unseen leaves, as they move
up the ridge through pools of moonlight,
and the thin shadows of branches
that swim across their backs
as they duck nimbly
and pass underneath the foliage.

Owls in the canyon chant from their monastery
in clefts of darkness locked away in secret.
Their voices remind us
of the hollowness in our throats
after the burial of a loved one
or downy light softer than water
that we seldom touch in the eyes of the dead.

I reach down to where the small
engines of insects whine in the dark place
under the duff of the forest floor
and touch the stars in their singing, touch
the clear stream in the throat of the moon.

Who believes me in all of this?

At the top of the ridge
in a clearing of trees,
one of the deer has stopped to look back.
Its large ears are translucent receptors
to any hint of fear.
Satisfied,
it disappears from sight.

I am

I am the solemn rose
lilting
between white foam,
and the egg.
I am the soft wave
breaking on the wing
forever;
between two summers,
and one winter.
I have tasted the salt
of birth,
of being
born,
of dying the death
in small hours.
I have crumpled
between the pages,
in the verse of absence.
I have been stricken
by a dream of living,
by a forehead,
by an elbow,
by a finger resting
on the Word.
I've spoken
to the broken syllables
of wind,
through the trees,
to this people,
who make up my parts,
in the past
and the future.

In these quiet hills

Silent stream rubbing sound against
boulders in the night. Water,
the falling of your clear gown
in the ravine, has taken a thimble full of eons
to touch smooth pebbles at the bottom.

Once the sea was here
in these quiet hills.

Shells trapped in dark mud,
harden into white hieroglyphics:
white memory traces of the sea.

Empire now laps at your hem
woven of dark trees and starlight.

Proud hills stand guard
and teach man your awful truth.

Let the falling leaf be his lesson.
Let the Ohlone basket woven of pine needles,
remind him of your gift.
Let him hold memories white traces
in the boned hand of his life.

Bruce Owens

Immense calm

An immense calm,
a sheet of translucent glass catching clouds
in its reflection; untamed depths
adrift with life.

Somewhere beyond the vast horizon,
the magic staff of a storm is touching the water
and this massive power is spinning
the calm into a roll of swells, a menacing looming
that causes nautical souls to quickly take down
the mainsail and lash it to the boom
and button down the hatch,
for the untamable sky and water is upon them.

Here, on the edge of the Pacific, I stand
on top of a cliff, where below, small waves
lull to shore, a thin stretch of beach,
and their small speech breaks quietly
in the sound of water. I listen into
the sound, as gulls fly overhead.
I am listening into each wave, trying
to comprehend their mysterious language;
the lisp of their speech.

Below, two women, caught in the green laughter
of their youth, dash along the wet sand,
leaving footprints, that are erased by the invasion
of eternal water, slipping in with a rhythm
that echoes the ghost centuries of time.

Inwardly, I smile, knowing the green flicker
of their laughter was my laughter, and their
youthful sprint was my sprint.

Sooner than they think the storm,
far out in the distance, will be upon them,

and they will fold their wrinkled hands on their laps
in the snug, water tight cabin, as a swinging lantern,
burns deeply with their dreams.

Bruce Owens

Tonight I want to sleep close to the earth

Tonight, I want to sleep close to the earth
where the snail crawls along the moist latitude of silence
carrying it's house around like a lantern of pale light.
I want to be found under the roses in the dark garden
glowing like a patch of moonlight. Here
the cat waits like a coiled spring ready
to surprise anything that moves out there,
and those eyes under the bushes
are two small globes of green fire.
I want the grass so close to my face
that each blade becomes a transparent window
slipping through the pores of my skin.

Old stone

North along the coast,
straight, clean dark
stings the air,
is strong with the musk-
rot of artichoke;
plowed fields
steeped in manure;
a fast blur;
headlights
rush out
attempting to tame
the old adversary night.

The pacific glows under the
Half moon of November.
The rains are late this year
as the northern hemisphere
tilts away from the solar rays
and enters the dead season of
the winter solstice. Soon
storms from off the Pacific
will lash at the coastline, rip
through forest, knock out electricity,
uproot homes in the rapids of flood-waters.

Tonight the ocean is polished smooth and is calm.

Waddell beach hunched with cliffs,
sits in silvered shadow;
the wet sand is a flick of thin light.
The creek glitters with tinsel,
swift channel that cuts
into the slap of waves: glass clean and cold.

95

Bruce Owens

Here there is no adversary to tame: nature is
entwined with nature and the ocean's
old motion is only the attrite will of order.

The ranger pulls into the sand lot and
blinds me with a high-powered searchlight
as he scans my car, then
the beam slides across the beach
intruding into every clump of shadow. Abruptly
the searchlight is cut off. No crime lingers here,
only a poet at night with his thoughts, the lone
cry of seabirds and the thin thud of waves.
His presence is enough for me.
I turn my car back out on the silent highway;
The wide tires hum to the stretch of black asphalt.

I pull off onto Swanton Road
And take the curves that twist up through the hills.
Moonlight through the branches of tall pine.
At Big Creek, I click off the hum of the big Chevy engine,
kill the headlights. The steel door slams shut against
the still of night. I want to listen
to the sound of water. Find comfort
in the dark. No thoughts follow me
down to the glide of the creek.
Alder, and sweet laurel lean together.
The branches twine to make a canopy, a secret cloister,
holy and ineffable. A small breeze enters like a prayer.

Up the road across a small bridge
Is where the old woman had lived.
The farmhouse still stands,
white stones mortared into walls
shine cold with the moon. Under the earth,

her eyes shine black like old stones,
testament to the body's finality,
the flaw that permeates time and is perfect.

In the field near the house, fallen logs of
Douglas fir are riddled with small tunnels
where beetles chew on the infinite repose of night.
A keen owl snatches the deer-mouse
in its beak and breaks all hope
of this small creature that thought to scurry from
those lidless globes of malice.

A weir in the creek flow creates
a flat pool, beyond that
the water eddies in the dark.
In the stillness of the pool,
Orion's belt shines.
I bring my eyes to this place. Above
the giant hunter drifts across the sky.
In the small hours before dawn,
he will drift past the trees high up
on the ridge and disappear.

At creek's edge, I place my hand
in the flow; the water is like
my lover's hair touched in dream
or like quick trout that slip through
the shadowy net of primordial wish
but the temporal penalties at this touch
inflicts my mind with the cold-real as I flinch
at the wet glide of the creek.
A breeze fills the upper branches of tall fir with surf-sounds;
the slender crowns toss
back and forth in the leeward elation.

Out in the creek, other old stones, slimed with algae,
shine inwardly with another night.
Weft of stellar glint scars the round cheeks
with glacial slip, eons of upheaval and drift,
the slow plunge of a continental plate
into the fire in the belly of
the earth, molten and hot,
this grind when time was young.

Sanderlings

In the edge of light, sanderlings
incessant chase of motion; waves
slip across sky-lit, sand-slapped wet.

The morning sprint on short stilts:
this little cavalry of Charlie Chaplin's
rush in perfect unity
across the shine
to the edge of a
retreating
lap
in the tilt
spin of earth.

All day long
these artic migrators
agile movement looms minutely from
the mirrors awash on Waddell beach.

The tongue of light
ripples the water at the mouth of the creek
swollen with late winter rain. On shore wind
sucked off the ocean, slips up the canyon slopes;
on the updraft, a hawk finds pleasure, and soars.

In the folds of the hills silence is bruised with shadow.
There is stillness that touches the shallow of the creek,
glitters in the mind, and is testament to
the small flock of *churring pritt,*
shy aggregate of three-toed feet
retreating in the edge of light: sanderlings
like so many humans,

Bruce Owens

a simple touch of white-breasted humor
scurrying in nature's traffic,
chasing the golden wave
that slips back towards the sun.

Landscape

I

I hear a train thundering up a spine of tree;
In the distance, as birds drop back into dead silence.
The clear complexion of night reveals a nest of stars;
As hands place early coins of chilled silver to my cheeks.

II

The northern wind fills my lungs with vapors of roads disappearing.
Clouds rise from below, where steam lingers above the Ohio River,
While drifts of fog stain the country landscape of wet rolling hills.

III

The green cowbell sways gently around the neck of wind.
On the sharp blades the grasshopper clicks his leg in the sun.
A fence along the road listens to the bark of dogs.

Our Bluebird Song

I wish I were a tree
to tie a string around your finger
to remember to wear a ring like water
Halo of evenings we carry through our lives
past the eyes of children in the garden playing
on the harps of clouds they dream
On our backs we dreamt that childhood passing
in the park with swings and slide and the green
leaves burned so brightly
as if to sing praise
For it all was praise and prayer
we just didn't hear it

To set the canoe adrift on the rippled mirror
of a lake in summer and glide under the lavender glow
as stars began to poke the sky
and to think in this moment I want to live
and never die

As autumn leaves gather at our feet
while a squirrel scampers up the tower of a tree
with the one window facing towards the sea
We have climb all these years to touch the bell
in the moment that disappears
from the upper sway of branches
like the wind that was the will of our life
now retired to a garden planting bulbs for spring
as we listen to the song in birds sing
our bluebird song

No trespassing

This yellow breast of fire
darts up on the wing
then dives down across the field.
A swarm of black birds move
magnetically as if driven by an unseen
force that fuses their flight into a pulse with purpose.
Just as suddenly, they land perfectly,
and perch momentarily on a telephone line.
The eyes follow a fence that twist up through the hills,
and is touched on top with barbed wire. Cattle country,
South County, No Trespassing.
The magpie, in all its grace, zips through
the invisible zone linked to the sign
shot full of holes.
This barbed wire reaches all the way back to Clear Water,
and keeps going until it rust
from traveling to long under the sun, and rain.

Too quickly

Your eyes never again can visit the countryside of your youth
when the streams ran clean, and your small feet
endured with joy the suck of mud at the waters edge
where bright things swam quickly through your sight
in that fast water more translucent than dream.
Too quickly this passed.
The tree-house swing,
and how she hung onto the two huge ropes,
leaning back as she kicked out over space,
and swung back up into the sky;
the old sycamore branch creaked lightly
with the memory of her weight,
and her squeal of joy quietly that disappeared on the wind.

Evening

In the shaded pools of the river,
where rocks gather for deep conversation,
The moss lit fins of Bass, disturb the surface of my dreams,
Causing ripples to reach the banks where deer come to drink.

Minnows

When I look up at the stars at night,
I have no bait
to catch them. They are
their own bright lure.
I don't have the tackle or
line strong enough to pull
them down from their
place in the sky. But when
I lean over
the edge of
a still tide pool, as if by
some chicanery,
there they are
caught in the simplest of mirrors,
these little minnows of light.

About The Author

Bruce Owens lives in Santa Cruz, California. He lectures on the nature of the creative process, and conducts poetry workshops, mainly with young adults, especially those struggling with addictions or who have come from abusive households, using poetry as an instrument of self discovery and as an entry into the world around us.

Acknowledgements

Some of these poems, in slightly different forms, have appeared in The Prairie Review, Indiana Voice Journal, William Everson: Remembrances & Tributes, and several previous collections to include Quiet Places, Eddies in the Rush, A Passage Through Stone, and Mend the Broken Branch.

Middle Creek Publishing Titles

Span
by David Anthony Martin

Deepening the Map
by David Anthony Martin

Phases
by Erika Moss Gordon

Cirque & Sky
by Kathleen Willard

Messiah Complex and Other Stories
by Michael Olin-Hitt

*Lessons from Fighting The Black Snake
at Standing Rock*
by Nick Jaina and Leslie Orihel

Wild Be
by One Leaf

Bijoux
by David Anthony Martin

Sawhorse
by Tony Burfield

Almost Everything, Almost Nothing
by KB Ballentine

Across the Light
by Bruce Owens

Kimono Mountain
by Mike Parker

www.ingramcontent.com/pod-product-compliance
Lightning Source LLC
Chambersburg PA
CBHW060401090426
42734CB00011B/2217